Dark Poetry, Volume 8: Tiptoe Thru The Twilight & Other Gothic Poems

Dark Poetry, Volume 8

J J Ginty

Published by J J Ginty, 2020.

DARK POETRY, VOLUME 8: TIPTOE THRU THE TWILIGHT & OTHER GOTHIC POEMS

First edition. June 24, 2020.

ISBN: 979-8201403317

Written by J J Ginty.

Also by J J Ginty

Table of Contents

Dedicated to the 'Isolationist':

Those who generally feel somewhat adrift

Those who perhaps feel they are something 'other'

Those who don't always believe in what is seen, heard, taught or disclosed

Those who are of a deep & introspective nature

Those who occasionally like to stick two fingers up at the external world

Those who are inwardly travelling Time.

In Appreciation. Always.

J J Ginty

I DREAM WITHIN THEIR DREAMS

I dream
I dream
I drown
I drown
With the untold
Countless paramours
Of old gentleman ghoul
& old lady fiend
Who fly above
Over Time
Who
Looking down
Into the black paralysis
See me drown
Within their dreams.

BEAST

O gusty wind upon shadowy mountain
I belong here, with you, nowhere
In desolation
In primal communion
Everywhere – an elixir in kindred blood
I feel it alone – only here
Lonely? – never!
Great moon
By you, I roar, I tear ... upon savage fold
So frail, so tender
The antelope
Hunted
I chase
To meet their death
Of this, I partake
'til the break in my fast
To conquer nothing
but to slake the drought in my blood.
These mountainous pastures
Where I rule,
for now,
It is only for now
Here, this moment ...
Possessed, spellbound
under your supernatural shadow

of moonlight
Where you & I are one/the same:
Same hunger, the same ... – irrevocable
In the end, I guess, I hope (no, pray),
that one day, in You,
I am freed.

AERIALS

Dream leaders supreme
Fraught with frozen heat
Pulsing pain
Delusion dashed
The transparent hedonism

Oh, it lacks, this earthly paradise
It's unending summer fair
Full of the flower, & the song, of those
Who grant to us the aerials of Plenty:
Hosts of ravishing wings

Eaters of bone & soul

The passions they bestow
Like a plague avalanche, sweet
Bitter their faces bleed, mutilations
Peeling & dripping onto their feet
Running from the flying wings of Paradise

The earthly leaders of Famine.

FOOTSOLES (INTO THE TWILIGHT)

Chasing my own fugitive footsoles
across the paltry pastures on into the twilight
of my own indifference on over the borders
which appear to snuff out the noise
of the murmuring sleeping birds
I feel their weighted eyes & folded wings
in the shadows, sleeping,
tho somehow watching over me
thinking again about life's sick philosophies
Watching, engrossed,
as all the engorged herds of frantic
babbling ghosts are being chased
all about me
by the lofty featureless Sandman
He is so blank, he is so struck & stuck
& tacked to the dead men who
are naturally cupped & chained
to the dream-men who have stolen
& are humping all of their stolen gifts
& dreams;
As I ride with these steely crooked phantoms
to ride onwards
to the head ... to The Crown –
to The Crown!

To see who will be crowned
To iron out the whole earthborn family
And to see all those who will shut down & burn
between these sleepy borders
which'll be roasting beyond the climes of Hell
in the Infernos at the impassable gorge
Where the Rulers will be emptying their Royal
accounts & affairs from under the noses
of their dying hungry domains –
The Sovereignties –
Where the Commoners & all of their families'
families' famished souls shall remain
ever earthborn,
waiting & waiting & waiting & ...
Waiting to break out from beneath
the white sandstone, limb by limb,
From under the tyranny
of this confused & savage noise.

SACRAMENT

November
portentous
melancholia
interned
beneath
stained glass
shivering
sunbeam
shines
vernal days
in the cold
tomb
of mourn
Solemn,
penetrating
Righteous ceremonious canticle
God-hearted, timorous &
Disgraced
by shameful
mortal powers
Enslaved
in error
– Mistakenly
Nailed to the brilliance
upon high

shining
Over sacramentalism's altar
where some priest
Is praying
For
My
Soul
?

OUTCRY

Broken
I leave
To follow
His footfalls
Out of dream
To stand
Naked
By his urn
Wailing
I slump
In Outcry
For all that was
His best
For all that was
His worst
Wanting
To listen
To his voice
Just once more
In Time
Wanting
To relive
Our dream
For always
Here

With me
Now
But only
In memory
Getting so much
Harder
To place him
To face him
As I turn
To fall
Once more
To the floor
I do wonder
What he would see
In me now?

SWEET THING

Her sweet minded thoughts
Kiss the pulse
The rhythm
Within the blood
What drums on
In the body
Thru me
From her

Oh, sweet minded girl

Who writes her mind
In the rain
The water of her soul
Beneath her moon
Upon my earth
A chance thing
A longing thing
To die again
& again
It's a Love thing

In this
Our place
Our sweet minded home

We share
The soul – our innermost
Personal space
To bring her life
Thru me
To breathe my life
From her ... Oh,

Sweet minded ghost.

DON'T STAY (I'LL NOT FORGET)

It's alright
Old friend
Everything comes
Everything goes
The pendulum swings
To equalize
All things

It's not our fault
There is no blame
We are all Angels, born
Of the eyes of shame
An intercession
Where we'll no longer need
For a day, or a night
To come

Don't wait for me
Don't stay
I'll be in no rush, nor haste
I have no need, nor desire
To be with you, together
Eternal
To be travelling
To somewhere that

JJ GINTY

You may or may not have gone

No
It is not for me
Not this time
I think, at least
Not yet, old friend
You are so close – too close
Please
… no need to stay
It'll be alright

I'll not forget.

LARAGHBRYAN

Rotting under a Millennia of unkept headstones
Molded, casted shapes & forms & names
Remembered – a cenotaph eulogizing Earth's ascetic bliss

I stare, breathing into the marble
Glowing upright in strength & Love
Come back, Sir, come back, or

Dare I climb in there ... with you?
Sir? ... to happier times – so simple, unattached – yet, not
With each passing perishable year

So fast – too fast – so soon – too soon ... Ice
Decorates the stuffed warm breeze with lugubrious woe
In this August vacation – summer – rain – humid.

You were, and still are, a Hero, to me, Sir. O brave individual
Formation, sinewy structure in aggregation, a figure of passion
Loyal, a flash of perfect human happiness gone

Too soon, Sir, too soon. You & I of intricate variegation, infinite
Intermingling lineage, bloodline, fadeless, in this darksome hour –
Here – where you rest – rotting – Here – only in name – Here –

Where I stare, breathing – a continuum of you – I lay this flower.

BABY DREAM

Smiling unhappily
Forever crowding in my moments
Into moments
Into moments
As another world drives on by
Seeing it all shot down, again

I'll keep on walking by, yes
But one day, I'll run
I'll fly – you'll see
Smiling happily because happily

All my problems shall be shared
When I never return here again
Swapping places to change faces
With all the many hundreds
The many thousands
Even the growing billions
Of ensuing unfilled newborns
Caught up in a half-light-limbo
Of their once-upon-a-previous ...
Now future memories

Oh, how I saw it all
When I was a baby in a dream

I dreamed about me
Being a baby in a dream
When I was some other baby
I was someone else's baby
Dreaming in *their* dream
Or was it in their memory
Reliving on thru me? Or

Some other body of magic
Who'll continue on
In some other memory's dream
Refilling their worlds
With my own little moments
Captured
Which one day may come to be
Crowding in the memory
Of my very own
Baby's dream?

THE PHOTOGENIC

The bottomless – unfathomable – early life
With all its inherited visions, which, I must suppose
are my dreams, I suppose, or could be
antecedent recollections, perhaps, of a dream
In some other cadaver's reality walking on thru
my waking-dream; the likes of such I call my life
This life – no longer early life – a dreamlike reality
Which, every day every night, seems to be
loitering on thru me
Tidal flows of arcane spell & mysterious hex
The wildest of past spirits
Who be the unthought of now my thought,
at least – so as I believe for now – it has to be me
Who sees all the unveiled secrecy swirling around –
In & around all & Thus & those who crowd from
underneath the stone urns – swirling, swirling
Swirling am I: this mortal solitude
in the overshadows
of ectoplasmic mist & ectothermic beams
To give rise to reveal all unscientific potentialities –
all non-possibilities – thru the now photogenic Orb
Where you can see the indestructible energy
in Hope's light
By your eye, in the lens, in the Light, thru me –
the 'backscatter' –

... see God?

MY, WHAT GREAT TEETH THEY HAVE!

I see it, I see it! My!
O my! don't they have great teeth!
I see them all, right there, biting
Biting at all the somebodies
... at all the nobodies
Biting
Even at the best of people
Oh, & some of the worst

Freezing their bones, chattering
Are their teeth, shivering
Where there is no more Sun, no more
Warmth, no coziness
Where y'can see some of these folk
(& where their backsides are to remain)
Sitting, frozen stiff
Where some lay stretched out & numb
Where so many have fallen
To remain

Where there are others ...
Who can ... well, kinda stand
I guess
Then just walk on by & away

Far off & away
Into the wilderness of no return

I think? into the recent dilapidations
Of new developments
Where the windy smokestacks used to bellow
Some kinda dirty black haze
That what used to be the great ships of
What was then (if I remember rightly)
The fantastic birth of contemporary imagination
To be gone
Up off into the once & forever, forever

Dream-filled nowhere skies
The very same horrifying once beauteous
Skies, which can now somehow in someway
Rip up & tear to self-create/recreate all by itself
Without my interceding assistance anymore, or
Any other kind of interference – none
Whatsoever – from my ancient order upon this

Their newfangled wilderness, as the nightly daily horror
Draws on in to engorge itself & then spits out as it lays
New grounds. Oh, what have I done
To these, all of these, so many, many of these?
Now all for the reckoning of
The new paupers who'll become the new princes
Who shall go on & on & replace them all & bury them
– frozen –
Into the vast & expanding cemented shipless oceans
Ready to make way for the newborn
Skippers & kings, impregnating their hookers & queens

Right there
Whom I can see, with their great teeth
Biting, biting, biting ...

I see it, I see it! Wow!
They really do have great teeth, don't they!
Oh, they do!
I see them all, right there, biting
Biting at all the somebodies
... at all the nobodies
Biting
Even at the best of people
Oh, & some of the worst ...

POPULATION: EXTINCT

Rising from their rest beneath
A cerement covered moon. Climbing
From out their beds, are the chattering
Leprous ghosts: chattering
About the cold & fireless days

Chattering about the craters created & laid
For more lepers to climb out of
And serve the Dark Lord
Under this, his shadow of this
Moon & cerement sky

Dwarfing the stone towns torn
Asunder to ignite the air & so fattening the sea
To swell upon thousands who drown echoing
Again ... & again ... & ...
Their voices of yore

These fleshless tireless bores
Who lay to rest to rest to rise & to rise
Evermore, to ever-walk
The sprawling shelled shores
That were once the walled streets of ...

POPULATION: EXTINCT

TIPTOE THRU THE TWILIGHT

Clear is everything wrapped in plump hunger-ridden preserve obliterating the thin meager light of victimless nightmare gray dream-reality

Where inter-dimensions remain beyond the Outlands behind generous nightly sapient screens of all knowledges

Thru which I can see destiny, all destiny, or is this my destiny: to continue extending the fake idiotic smile of courtesy to those gray answerless men behind cosmetic faceless renovations of no discernable impression?

Who so bring to me their materializations of Oblivion

Who so strangle & choke the matriarchal air out of all life out of all the babes who know nothing but of Id, of God, & of humble Eternity:

The great cock making its great love infinitely thru the great vagina of Time – eternal orgasm

Spawning endless life, never-ending, with no possible beginnings outside Mind's conceptions of the Big b-b-bang-bang-Bang of well researched organized lies becoming theory to become Fact, and so complete, but Truth is never Complete.

Ever truly realizing this

As I writhe & roll around, incapable, in this refinery of the fermented spirit that trembles amid the storm of agony, clutching onto a shaky drink hand with the skinny drop-dead body of a lifeless weed

Whereupon bloodless yellow-white skin ripples the unreal river over ribcage, heart, casting out the stinking breath's precious last sigh ... inhumes the penniless cheerless eye

Seeing past every single ray of wretched hope, all withered but for a little poisoned charity upon the bibulous tuneful tongue, which is so guiding me to the soothing cool fountain glittering where there is no fear, no, not in here

As together we drown in Peace Love & all things good & all things true ... or not!

Whereby our futures are to be split right in two by this distilled shaking of hand ensuring that we (that is you & me) are completely out of our hideous heads, broke

Once more as we rip & tear at ourselves & one another, along with any other, like some kind of juiced-up drug-crazed human-hybrid-chimpanzees.

Or, maybe ...?

Yes, maybe, I should just keep on tiptoeing right on thru – recording how much this all fucking hurts! – listening to all the useless piss-drunken verbosity. There is too much verbosity! I should know

For I have to spew enough of it out of myself in some vain aim to try and keep up with all

Those who read my words and listen to my voice within the deaf brainless acoustics of their own mind's ear: those who never truly say what they ever truly mean

For fear that the irretrievable Word might foam from their smelly shit-stained lips puckering their way thru the subterranean back passage and so exposing their weird labyrinthian folds of massive Ego

Bungling thru relics of opinion made somehow anew, embellished from out of the old ... from out of their own rebirth thru untouchable converse

– Top Secret –

As if God himself sanctioned such an enormous cloudburst of dung-dust to hail down upon us

As we breathe, ingesting digesting, violating you, violating me, having their own way with us, ensuring that we leap to our own fall, so steep, peeling back the lids of our own coffins to look way down deep so deep

Inside to reach around and give ourselves our very first handjob – like it's truly something new and should be ever so fucking grateful for

While their empty bribes just keep on growing on up out of the melting human ice, reflecting the falling cleft skies off rising comets like no other spectacle ever seen before the end of Time

Showing us the way to forget all about ourselves, so as to become *themselves* thru false memory, masquerade, word and gesture

In their 'all new' bright & shiny eugenic plastic world performance

Just so they can give us all of that which we now Hate, unconditionally, just as they so took from us all of that which we once Loved.

And O how I see them loom,

As this naked solitude of self-communion releases me all the way up out of my temporal shackles – all the way up into the Nothing –

From that which is the deluded purpose of my own company & my own best friendship, vainly pondering

On how the now prevailing corrupt ambition bedeviled & scourged the once sacred today houseless temples in monolithic cities of the ancient past – that which is disappeared –

Taking with them the cyclopean hypocrites: those who most unashamedly & unrepentantly return again

And again, from the dark Dark Ages with the topmost stupidest of wonderings, revolting in their iniquitous clusters of gregarious bodies, stomach-churning in their meandering & chuntering from their hermitic gaga minds – bedazzling one & all

& even more with their feigned miracles – or is it illusion? – nobody cares!

And why should they care? for the heart wants what the heart wants in this Age of Entitlement (not Enlightenment) as long as the ministerial department of dogma go on resurrecting the dearly beloved's bruised & battered souls

Those who are unschooled in the rottenness of sober truths: that which may lead to the purest & foulest of Temptation – Genocide!

Ever swimming around, snorkeling on thru the blood red sea in the
cardinal slimy stench of the utmost sincerest human action, preceded by
the utmost earnest & caring & loving fanatical human Thought
Which is almost always stolidly fixed in its own way upon Heaven &
all its dessertspoons feeding baby goop to aggrandized disciples ever
wanting for more & more & more & ... O please!
Can't y'all just give it some more? ...
More misanthropy
More Holy order
More of that "Whatever!" feeling
More absurd purpose
More renouncement
More earthly ambition
More of this that & the other
More double standard
More Thought Police
More weaning off the Mind/the Soul
More proselytization
More false hope
More great charm
More further from the Truth
More besides
More judgement, more puerile conceit, more extravagant hyperbole &
more ...
Napalm – more IEDs
More retribution
More lab-created disease
More germs – more pesticides
More genetically modified
More highs – more lows
More dystopian dysphoria
More liquor – more drugs

More gossip – more media
More never-ending bullshit
More laws – more restrictions
More contradictory equality
More political correctness
More autocratic democracy
More mob-minded rule
More humanity thru vanity
More brainwashed apes
More make-believe reality
More televisual screens displaying
More exploitation
More pornography
O come on!
Please!
Can't y'all just give it some more? ...

... For nothing to ever change
Though Nothing *is* ...
Eternal change
In Time – perhaps
Where we (that is you & me)
Can cut some other great deal
In some other Great Space ...

... Until then,
Clear Mind
Open Soul
Breathe free
Relax.

ANESTHESIA

Seeing how everything seems to pass
In just the same old crippling white blindness
Numbness in-between excitable doings
At her controls controlling my pain is
Anesthesia. O sweet, sweet Anesthesia!
As I lay here
Paralyzed
In quasi-junk euphoria
Pupils dilating
My vein pulsating
Bulging for her: my soothing naked nurse
In her cute little body caressing uniform clinging to her
& eating her all up
The delicious pain that feeds her
To palliate me
Propping her up in her own shadow's fragile sense of muted self-existence
Against the unloving impossibly sterile walls of Purpose
& Belonging here
With me to take from me – not just me – just scarcely enough
Pain from All
To get her thru too much: that which she cannot cope with
Needing more – always needing more
Like some kind of unselfish whore – a slave to it:
The Pain Junky
That's who she is

With her needles & drugs, pills & potions
Getting high
Addicted
& feeling Real
On pain
Reminding her
In all this suffering
Like it or not
She's alive.

O sweet, sweet Anesthesia!

CANNIBALIZED

Hanging in the general paresis of that which is in the idiot gas stinking up the whole place like a ruptured sewer spilling out death extract all over my face

My thoughts from the deserted outskirts of the pure & irrigated minds

Handing me used old pictures from the outhouse of before:

The jewels of terror which are by someway supposed to be a true likeness, a true representation of various turnstiles in my fragmented haunted youth

Snapping at the gaseous decay leftover from overdose, leftover from the fishy girl smiles, leftover from the dirty monkey shit twists in my suffering pleasure:

All the dirty things creeping beneath the skin broken down within this now terminal naked flesh excrement

In the sloughs of the lovelust orgasm in the diseased heavenly odors in filthy frightened dirt fuck city

And recalling all the frantic suffocating smells: I recall the dying death tissue and the daily uncontrollable act, the daily degenerate routine of spitting up blood-mucus from the soiled Being

The soiled Being who goes on hiding his adolescent scars behind what's left of his boyish face

By which he hangs, as he views his disgusting reality projecting his morbidly sick terminally sick dipsomania thru his kaleidoscopic eyes blinded by the sodden brown drenching paranoia that peels its way into my vacant pants –

The impotent dead pants & the cold stale encrusted urine spattered all about my spontaneous portable pissoir
My nerve-endings now shattered & split in this crude gray circumstance – my cold gray alien bones in ragged trauma, in earshot of the taunting laughing to be heard within the sing-song shadows: singing my name, my Name … I'm gonna think me up another new name – that'll fool 'em for a while!
Marinating in the whiskey-glazed breath from my moldy old smelly cigarette teeth & my smoked-out eyes that burn & squirm – I am polluted –
To the stomach, to the liver … & beyond –
Watching this gray flesh from within my body drip from the ceiling gallows – cuffed & noosed – to the floor
Being milked by these, my life's unendurable revolting final images, chanting chunks of brain in stalactite bondage
Where I be hanged – cannibalized –
By this
My true likeness of which
I shall no longer have to abide.

IT

Speaking inside
Thinking deep
Inside
My internal footslog
Mournful trudge
Without hope
Not even
A little hope – No

No
I'm not ready for it
For it to happen
To be buried, forgotten
Under this here tiny stone
Beneath these chambers
Of conflict
The inner house
Of feeling

To only look back at life
To ever look back at him
At him! whom I never was
To catch a glimpse of once (maybe twice)
At whom & what he or I could have been

No
I'm not ready for it
Not yet, not for that
I'm too busy
Speaking
Inside
Thinking deeply
Wondering – with little hope:
When *it* does come – when *it* does happen
Then quite possibly
I can be freed
Then most probably
I could end this –
My internal footslog
My mournful trudge –
And live?

MOVE ON

Born of the biochemical waste
The dismal Karma
The cancerous foe
He knows no enemies, he has none

At the top of the food-chain
Where their petty arguments lead
To the bullet
The bullet in the brain

The Allies outrage
Suggesting "we have won!"
And the 'winning'
Is all but everything

Even after
The body-count is done
Forever pictured
In the galleries

The galleries of our dismal Karma
All hanging
In the now budding, flowering
(Once killing)

J J GINTY

Red on green fields
For all of our Nations' hurt
"Lest We Forget"
But learn not the lesson

Bury our children
And move on.

ART

The longing hunger of the once fat now flat bellies, stiff, propped up before the stronghold of talented cruel weasels,
The serpents, the foraging grubby hogs, the rabid dogs
Who, morphing their ugly empty meaningless abuse into the chauvinistic headlines that
Headline the unreal – into the real – giving rise to the oppressive nimbus battalion
Who, so saint-like, march on out of their own sordid bad dreams to menace at the still flowering source of the perennial tenacious meek
Who, brandishing their superhuman sabers in yet another knife fight
Cutting down the old thinkers & crones & hags & magicians

Who, so brightly feathered, still pass on their mindless minds of ageless age so effortlessly
In vain, attempting to hide from the all-viewing eye of the perfectly colored eyes, skin hair, of the saintly nimbus people.
These are the *real* people
Who dare (but do not want) to set forth their raw-boned foot from inside the dying simple forest –
By force –
To step into & live on ... to become dumbshow in a god-blessed so-called free world:
A quintessential paragon depicted thru surfeit art

That does so inventively convey The Millennium of oppressing this long, longing hunger.

THE LADDER

Like Hell it is
Living
Living the disaffected
City life. Oh, my!

From out of this Hell

Take me
Take me
Take me

Up the ladder
Up to the toppest tops
Above all this

Away from the loneliness
The loneliest
Crowds – this population
Where the people

Are all Hell
It's one thing, Hell
And that is, people
Yep, people are Hell

That's right – that is so
And I ain't gonna be struggling no more
Under the carrying of this old ladder
Over the hustling heads & the bustling shoulders

Of these people
These ever so busy people – the way too busy people
No more – nope
I'm gonna set it right down and climb

Right off the ledge
Onto the rungs – climbing
Right up to the very top of
Wherever it may lead

Yep, no more so-called big living for me
No more City – no more living
As one of these – or as one of those
Everywhere, living

In Hell
In the overpopulation
Amongst the overcrowds
One of the disaffected

– The lonely people.

THE LUXURY

I remember
that
she loved me
more than any woman
has ever loved
a man
before

I remember
how
she hated me
more than any woman
has ever hated
a man
before

I remember
then
how I bathed
in her lifeforce
her eternal essence
in the utmost unholiness
of our pain

My suffering

in her Luxury
of the likes of which
she shall never
be remembered
again

ALONG THE INDIAN HIGHWAY

As I travel the road along the Indian Highway,
the highway into sickness and ultimate death –
ultimate …? well, cosmic consciousness I suppose
Along the road to where the cosmos is restrained
against its will by the most electrifying
of purest screams
That seem to fill up my tangled head everywhere
from out of everyone's feathered head
into my saxophonic mind
Playing their old stories & testimonies for me
motioned in their antediluvian blues –
Some early rumbling melodies that guide me thru
their past visions:
The prophetic phantoms,
with their motheaten old senile faces masking
their now ancient certainly no less than mortal
minds
I suppose … for me …
in this, their shuddering little performance,
their little madness prairie stage, in this small
lonely jewel of a dream school
Re-enacting the brave decorations of old
Indian Chiefs slaughtered by the armies
of shady old European germs:
The revolutionary idiots with industrialized

powers of depression, modern anxiety, illness,
very short hair, beards, liquor & a new kind of
killing, death, fear ...
To be bled, impregnated & bred into Mankind's
tipis & wigwams of ultimate consciousness
Scattered all along this now scalped highway,
& all over what was once an unrestrained,
courageous & untainted, born to be free,
barebacked crosslegged wonderland.

THE TOUR GUIDE

As he was rolling his cigarette – smoking his herb –
A troop of cartoons enter – out of mirage –
one-by-one – immediately
Picturing unusual thoughts – elaborate
Astronautics – the ancient celestial beings
– unintelligible – highly advanced –
glyphs & symbols by Mayan settlers – I think;
As explained to me by this asshole broker – stoned
Goggling out from his wonky lensless glasses
Who'd had a drink or two –
considerably screwed – I'd say
A bit young in the trousers
to know about these things
Silently laughing,
he points to his green jism stains,
right there in the sand
– y'understand? –
all next to a hairy perspiring
human compost heap
Which appeared to have
some rare marijuana growing
along with the mushrooms
from out of his ears
I could see all these smells twitch,
as he began to fry up before

the swarms of ravening flies
under the unforgiving
Mexican sun. Oh, & not forgetting ...
How he decoded the unique codices,
apparently authored out of his ripe
& dangerous vomit, & his septic flesh,
hereby mummifying
these once animated artifacts
To reveal unto me
a load of characterless, headless,
depraved hairless monkeys, erect,
stoned, in clay bastardized markings
Whilst he laughed & continued to sup
from his fake little pottery cup –
Quaffing it all right down
on into his fermenting rotting gizzard –
Some more of his illegal
"medicinal" piss. (Fun & games, what?)
It was all so terribly disappointing!

OBITUARY

Necrologies of assembling Buddha-like corpses walk the graveyard canyons in the misty smog ozone with the starveling skulls, looking for a nourishing meatless sandwich, that's all, or ... something like that, I think, I am hungry too?

Starvelings! with our corpses waxed into Man's inane notions of fixity, we are bearing the cross of the wizardly Universe: evermore black, yet, thru the uncloaking of Time, forevermore, transparent.

In-coffined (but so uncommonly blessed) am I (& always have been) throughout this half-century

With all of those (& we, & me, & you) who, malnourished, in these pale echoing decades remain truly Ignorant – divorced from our so-called 'understanding' – but with wisely hands that still wave to the phantoms in the full moon whilst smoking our immortal soul's gleam out of our eyes like old chimneys, stoned, in the empire of municipal life

And, with them would-be necrophobic Bodhisattvas everywhere, earning themselves some kind of Karmic merit on the bus ride that never terminates,

Passing metal cars – flying vision, dream, achievement, acquirement –

Driven by the very long beards, accompanied by the very short hair

Steering metal into the face of Destiny (never what it used to be)

As the fellow replicants' footsteps beat down upon the multiplying (over-inhabited) sidewalks where some now beg, hoping to rebuild bellies from years ago

Hurling up abuse at the street sheriffs, lofty in their haste, their pursuits – O how Justice imparts! –

Forgotten by the years of 'training' – all brainwashed now –
Here, where my not so "a fond farewell" leaves the bleak rising over kindly swollen-headed dolls:
Empty phantomless eyes of all varying class that stare spittingly at me
A sign of how it's always been
In the upstairs of empty narrative – paragraph after paragraph onto chapter onto ...
Maybe singing me a verse – perhaps a chorus – maybe even two
To be then written on up ... into the latest ensemble – into the Globe's eternal obituary.

SCHOOL'S OUT

Nightfalls

Laying its final hand on my face
Suffocating me
Simultaneously
My bald head glistens
Now transfigured

I was christened (I think?)
Before all this began
The unsightly thing to drown
Again & again
From foot-to-head

Very ill-bred
Way to create the omnipotent Shadowman
Out of books & songs
& other such things

School is out
Was is it ever even in?
Probably
It was just me that wasn't in – right?

J J GINTY

Watching my own eyes now beaming floodlights
Stretching right out across the midnight fallen skies
Blinking (unknowingly) upon this Kingdom
& over my consecrated, so faithfully dedicated
Soon to be ordained

Travelling companions,
Returning
Winking
(ever so knowingly)
Back at me.

POKER

Finally
Revealed
From behind
The poker-face
The whole damned wretch
Who
All-night, all-life, all-time
Long time … swinging
The useless pickax
Mining this soul
I groan
Forever owned – No
Not forever – No
How can that be?
Who knows?
Really knows?
Finally
Breaking out of this old
Thought Creation
The familiar safe
Prison of Reality
& all its chitter-chatter
Thru the one-way
Conversations
The blah-blah-blah

Vacuous
Conversations
That ride the mind
Alone & bluffing
My way thru that
What really rolls
This sinking boat
Is soon to bring
The empty vessel
To the poker-game
Where I sit alone
Among the hearts of gold
Crippling cold
For they too alone
Finally reveal All
In just that one, blinding
Phantom-disrobing
Singular moment, Just before
We *all* leave the room.

"TO PROTECT and TO SERVE"

Settling beneath the big things
The lights that roll on thru the night
Every night – all night
Long into what goes on
Beneath the rooftops, the streets

Within all the crashing to be heard
Giving all a sense of want & worth
Less the realization of the unbearable
Sinking sickness of the life killing life & soul
Searching, groping for the madness of sanity

The gimmick of the waste-paper-basket-mind
Lusting to go out hunting for some busted heads
Just so as to bust up some more heads
Then, to brag about it
And all that has been achieved throughout

The night of another night for another
Giving cause to be effective in not telling the truth
(to lie in other words – yes, that's right – lie) "Your Honor"
About what we've been really doing
Every night for over two-hundred years

JJ GINTY

So as to pave out our way for our way back home – slowly, drunk
& pretty exhausted, as usual, trying not to kill ourselves along the way
Tho we'd be better off gambling it all away
To then hopefully be buried by someone who at least
Pretends that they care

But, instead, we go on to get married to have our children
Grow up beneath the big things, beneath the rooftops
To continue the legacy, the reputation, the service & the honor
Of what must be perjured under the clear hidden view of the lights
Of the red & blue flashing lights that roar to roll on thru the night.

THE MADMEN

... blowing my nose into the germ-stained handkerchief of over 7 billion dreams into the bacteria Apocalypse governed under the illusions & delusions of madmen Pentagon Juntas:

Genetically recombinant hypnotized human-alien zombies who'll never stop radiating their infinite neutron beams paralyzing not so motherly nature's flyblown ulcerous genitals

All behind the naked incontinent asspiece that keeps on shitting newspaper headline excrement into the dirty old toilet of snide insults, smearing, campaigning, wiping & washing the blood guts & lives away with their own perverted gossamer of The Ten Commandments

Washing it all away & up into the green crucified realm, into the nowhere, way off up into the polluted ether of weightless abstract light, painting infinite memory of Grudge forever to be – to be Forever

Bullied & oppressed by the police messiah, the armies of superdicks rising up out of the death-squad-horizon beating their western & eastern drums of carnage with the music-sticks of buried children's mummified bones that mobilizes their self-fulling prophecies

Recorded in the plasma of lost nostalgia dripping down from the vermillion sky into my eye that burns in the near 8 billion flames

Which sears infinite memory forever etched into my denuded old grandfather mind

Staggering, stripped, naked, angry in the dynamo heaven of drunken purgatory

Blinking, listening, observing, vomiting, drowning in every nations' horror & lies

Pictured for you me & for all to see to view in the myriad madhouse vegetable museums
Where I do weep under the rule of the degenerate ecstasy of salvation's innumerable pubeless joyrides
Twisted! right from out of the pitiful wretched dreams of pederast patrolmen who, from time-to-time, get caught off duty with the madmen's help copulate their way back into the womb of the wailing sirens
To remain unchained mortal cacodemons, protecting & serving the giggling High who overlook juvenile cemeteries, scattering & burying more self-perfected skeletons to keep jobs for the foghorn coke-smashed loudmouthed brain-laundering & whitewash Agencies
Broadcasting themselves throughout the land via the sweet honorable somehow lyrically artistic face of their gallant & heroic smarmy household charm
No, of course not, not from out of their semen-stained blood-poisoned underwear but thru the cleaned & laundered baby-kissing mouthpiece of the criminal White Paper rulers
Who play with whatever they like to play with whomever they like to play with under the all-powerful protection governed by the multinational crosseyed sentinels
Those of whom we love to cheer for, whom we love to celebrate & applaud for, as they take laud for themselves, ringing out the old to ring in the new Caesars of our world
All of those whom we pay for with our very lives for their floats parades & motorcades
Where they do so generously & regally wave to us, grinning thru their clubbable masks, at the same time hiding away is their first-class manifold, never to be revealed to be seen, true & multinational face of the madmen identity
Who are to be hereby driven around & 'round at their own leisure – All at Life's cost – at All of Man's expense

In their blacked-out super-bulletproof soul-stained world-devouring globally dominating two-faces-for-the-price-of-one, so shiny & hearse-like, presidential automobiles.

THE HUMAN FARM

Mystical winds,
Smelling of human gas,
The fucking human animal farm!
I'm here choking & puking in what seems to be
everyone else's shit
In that what seems to be haunting the whole
goddamned Earth
From pole-to-pole
Terrorizing every well-meaning nostril
that dares to sniff at what used to be the
clean fresh air – man, it was so good for you
back then!
Oh, the once boundless intellect
Now the chuntering idiotic manure
that passes as fuckin' brains!

IN "CULTURED SOCIETY"

In a body of cesspool
amidst all the hers
& all the his
grinning genitals
bulging & leaking caviar
into cum smudged
moist panties, laughing
yakety-yak-yakkin'
into bathing suits
birthday suits
receding topcoats
stuffin' & chokin' each other
with the most exorbitant
living bullshit on show
'round their pulsing
screeching hoary necks
twisted
pseudo happy jovial cocaine
tongues flappin', chops lickin'
slaverin' up on all sides
in the body of cesspool
the fat green vulture piss
of high society's covetous
clown feet staggerin'
this way & that

in sick neon vapor
trippin' over their own assholes
& mores
All in the name of ultimate conversationalism.
I can't believe my fuckin' ears sometimes
Even less, my eyes!
To try and preserve society's 'cultured' personality
has gotta be the ultimate ugliness in vulgar vanity.

CHRISTMAS EVE

Christmas lights glisten along death's doorways
Grimy shivering collars old & worn in the fetid grease
Precinct shopping trollies vagabonds volte-face dreams
Of new days new ways as new year approaches
My dear give us a kiss right now for now
I'm right back in the nineteen-ninety's
Crumpled memory-sick blues that ventilate my face
In this pantomime of no surprise
Stealing nothing but imagination
In a hackneyed world so neatly packaged
Into one size fits all seasonally wrapped
& perfectly housed
In Caucasian eyes
All kinds of eyes
Call & collect
This time of year
To reassemble
To reunite
Every living lifeless
Godless apostate
Infidel eye
For the Christ's sakes

But not for *our* souls' sakes

O not this year my dear
On this Christmas Eve
Lights glistening grime
In precinct cold
Doorway alone
Shivering old
Worn
Fetid & greasy.

THE HUMAN GIFT

Blight, contagion, unnumbered ills
God's bloodhounds – His ennobled beings
Outspread their quenchless fires
Bearing down upon the slaves – the victorious
Lions of misery
Affording Man – the body
The taintless Mind – poisoned
In the fevered veins
Disease, junk & crime.
Gather 'round, folks!
It's all here, right here – consumed
Drinking in the void of despair
Transient – I devour Eternity
A child of terror – a gift
Enshrined in feeble song
Of fleeting sapient impulses
& scar-lines echoing in the drunken vaults
The necessary voyage thru renovated spirit
In the clear calm of Nature
A True God's human gift
Without the cry of ministrant avarice.

O CHILD OF HEAVEN

Here,
beneath swirling wreaths of clouds
– these elegant coronets –
I am refreshed, reborn, a child again
Nestling in the snug delicate clusters
– long gone – which linger
Unaccompanied
Somewhere, drowsing, half-lost
Somewhere
Where Time
interchanges & exchanges
with my nimble thoughts
Rippling along this budding stream
of innocence
Down by the riverbanks
of yesteryear
Where it's all the same
as it once was
Downward
Smiling into the carefree
Riverbeds,
as deep as an ocean
but without the turmoil
– Diffuse –
In the Oneness of my colossal psyche

Propagating beyond any miserable murk
Here,
where I still wilt
under these
foliaceous shelters
The shades,
which are nowhere,
chasing beyond
The luxuries of my earliest horizons
On into the fantastical light
& beyond
the great darkness
Which is all here
(in virtue of me)
– a child again –
Caught up in this leafy watery Heaven.

FIRST LOVE

Running rivulets of poetry
Throughout mortality
The immortality
In God's pastureland
Where I couldn't care less
Whether my voice
Can express
The sun be hot
Or the rain be cool
Or whether
The unoppressed birds
Do fly
Beyond the high
Concealing my silly
Beer-glass smile
In Elysium's grassy
Everlasting vistas
Where my grazing
Soul
Increases
Growing
Augments
Where the lines run on & on
& on
In me, thru me

Poetry
Nature's first language
Love's first love of
Original human language
Which is spoken thru All
Throughout Everywhere
In Everything.

PROPOSAL

Cloistered in His transforming kiss today
Life's perfect ardor in my obedient Surrender
That sees into Origin's original proposal
Thru His tender vocal in the garden bird singing
To me, my neighbors, and one & all about
The things in my life
For those who are listening
For those who care – the rare who share
The One Being
In fathomless cradle rocked by cosmic maids
In higher spheres – who knows?
But today, I Believe
For today
At least
I am kissed.

HIS VOICELESS UNWRITTEN POEM

Divine
is the Incarnate,
but the body
circumscribes
the endless Mind
Lacking substance,
without nucleus,
ungardened
is the Lord & mine
That conceives
the holy perfume,
which translates from
the consecrated grave
of the flesh
to the lightening
of endless Mind
Dissolving in the
infinite structure,
the answerless Eternity
at the moment of Earth's
great anointment
Thru Him,
to be spoken –
His lexicon –
Everlasting –

in the wordlessness
in all of that
which He unveils
Between the lines
The stanzas
within His voiceless
unwritten poem.

PRAYER

O heavenly lands beyond the utmost privations,
Holy Order
& the disciplines of Saints

Beyond all such tendencies & Mind-believing motives
In a world in which most cling absurdly to Promise
Supposing to enter a more devotional conception
Perhaps, in the Glory of whom the eye is not yet to see.
Which eye?

O sober Father eye of naked mindedness of Age
& of miracle
Who have dwelt in all God in all Being in all Flesh
Of all Heart & of all Soul in beginningless endlessness
Beyond all prayer & all meditation

Where You abide – Abba –
In my deepest, inmost reflection
For You, O timeless soul of the closed lip & open heart

Amidst this
My mist of rhyme
In all of this
Which does not rhyme

A mere gist
To form a list
In line
Splicing line
In word
Dicing word
My poem
My prayer.

Don't miss out!

Visit the website below and you can sign up to receive emails whenever J J Ginty publishes a new book. There's no charge and no obligation.

https://books2read.com/r/B-A-CIXC-YDVGB

BOOKS 2 READ

Connecting independent readers to independent writers.

Also by J J Ginty

Dark Poetry
Splinters
Dark Poetry, Volume 2: Gothic Twilight.
Dark Poetry, Volume 3: Views From A Gothic Window
Dark Poetry, Volume 4: Gothic Twilight II
Dark Poetry, Volume 5: Gothic Twilight III
Dark Poetry, Volume 6: Gothic Twilight IV
Dark Poetry, Volume 7: Gothic Twilight V
Dark Poetry, Volume 8: Tiptoe Thru The Twilight & Other Gothic Poems

About the Author

J J Ginty is an eclectic writer who is indeed a poet by nature and selection; and beautifully exhibits his artistry through the composition of verse and prose. An author who could perhaps write about any theme in any place, in any time, or any space. Composing his work to suit almost any style, and almost any taste. Having a propensity towards the darker characteristics of life (and death); whether they'd be real or surreal; natural or unnatural (supernatural); normal or paranormal; ordinary or extraordinary. It would be difficult to sum J J Ginty up as a writer; but for now, at least, it shall be said ... he is a writer/poet who has crafted his style to articulate the Dark and the Gothic.